D1257530

The Great Breakfast Book

NORDIC WARE®

$\mathcal{N}ordic\ \mathcal{W}are$ products have become a central icon in many American kitchens. In fact, every 4.5 seconds a Nordic Ware product is purchased somewhere in the world. Nearly 60 million Bundt® pans are in use, and the number continues to grow with an extensive new line of Bundt® shapes added in recent years.

Founded by H. David and Dorothy Dalquist in 1946, Nordic Ware remains family-owned and dedicated to providing outstanding customer service and support for their great innovative kitchenware products. Nordic Ware's commitment to inventing and re-inventing its line of American-made cookware, bakeware, microwave and barbeque products is paralleled only by the company's commitment to the community, its customers and employees and maintaining its "family" atmosphere. The company recognizes customer satisfaction with its quality products is the basis for continued success, and as a result, Nordic Ware enjoys enormous customer loyalty. The company has stood the test of time from its inception in 1946, to its recent transition from middle class marvel to gourmet comfort food status.

Although the company's first products were ethnic bakeware products such as the Rosette Iron, Ebelskiver Pan and Krumkake Iron, Nordic Ware is best known for its Bundt® Pan. It was after a large baking competition in 1966 where the winning recipe, the Tunnel of Fudge cake, was baked in a Bundt Pan, that the popularity of the Bundt Pan among the general public skyrocketed.

With **The Great BREAKFAST Book**, Nordic Ware proudly delivers a selection of recipes that vary from tried-and-true classics to wild flavor combinations that will surprise your guests and liven up any breakfast offering. Many of the recipes in The Great Breakfast Book are kid-friendly, suited for children's assistance during cooking. All of the recipes in this book can be made with a few simple items found in every kitchen, and ingredients from your local grocer. Happy cooking!

Contents

Waffles

Eggs

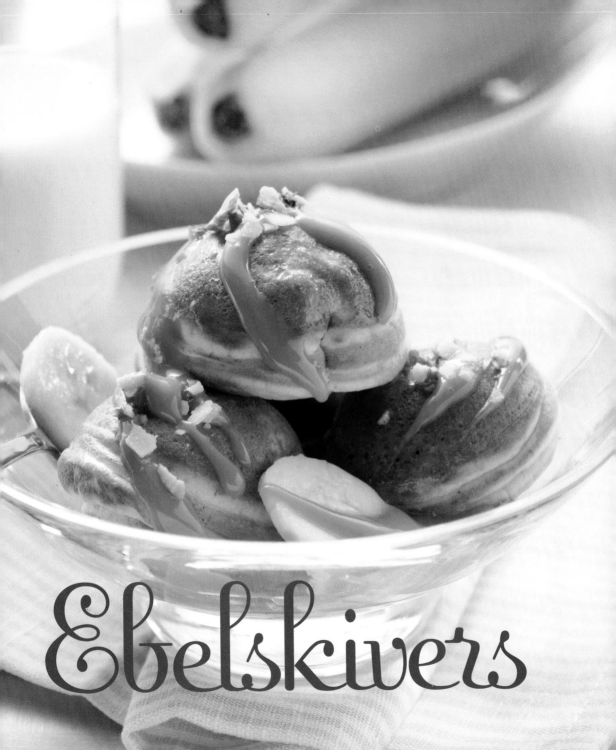

Ebelskivers

DANISH
Ebelskivers

BASIC BATTER

prep time 15 min
cooking time 24 min

makes 21 *ebelskivers*

3 large eggs, separated

2 tablespoons sugar

½ teaspoon salt

2 cups (250 g) unbleached all-purpose flour

1 teaspoon baking powder

1 teaspoon baking soda

2 cups (480 ml) buttermilk, shaken

2 tablespoons (30 g) butter, melted

Method

1 Beat egg yolks with sugar and salt.

2 In a separate bowl, whisk together the flour, baking powder and baking soda.

3 Add dry ingredients to the yolk mixture alternating with the buttermilk.

4 In a separate bowl, beat egg whites until stiff peaks form. Gently fold egg whites into the batter with a rubber spatula.

5 Heat ebelskiver pan over medium heat until hot. Pan is ready when a small amount of water sizzles when sprinkled over the pan.

6 Brush pan with a little butter and heat until it begins to bubble. Fill each cup ⅔ full of batter.

7 After 3 to 5 minutes, turn ebelskivers using wooden chopsticks or skewers and cook for another 2 to 3 minutes until browned on all sides. Repeat using all the batter.

Note

This basic batter is used in many of the other recipes or can be enjoyed on its own, dusted with confectioners' sugar.

CHUNKY BANANA TOFFEE
Ebelskivers

prep time 20 min
cooking time 28–35 min

makes 21 ebelskivers

3 tablespoons dark molasses

¼ cup (60 g) butter (½ stick)

⅔ cup (200 g) sweetened condensed milk

Salt

2 bananas

Juice from ½ lime

1X basic batter

½ cup (60 g) chopped pecans

2 tablespoons (30 g) butter, melted

Sea salt flakes

Method

1 In a saucepan, combine molasses, butter, condensed milk and a pinch of salt. Simmer over medium heat for 8 to 10 minutes while stirring constantly. Let toffee sauce cool.

2 Peel bananas, cut into small cubes and marinate in the lime juice. Toss diced bananas with 1 tablespoon toffee sauce. Set aside.

3 Prepare basic batter (see page 8).

4 In a pan, toast chopped pecans and stir into the basic batter.

5 Heat ebelskiver pan over medium heat until hot. Pan is ready when a small amount of water sizzles when sprinkled over the pan.

6 Brush pan with a little butter and heat until it begins to bubble. Spoon 1 tablespoon batter into each well. Place 1 teaspoon banana-toffee filling in the center and seal with 1 teaspoon batter.

7 After 3 to 5 minutes, turn ebelskivers using wooden chopsticks or skewers and cook for another 2 to 3 minutes until browned on all sides. Repeat using all the batter and banana-toffee filling.

8 Drizzle ebelskivers with toffee sauce and sprinkle with sea salt flakes to serve.

APPLE STRUDEL
Ebelskivers

prep time 1 h 15 min
cooking time 28–35 min

makes 21 ebelskivers

½ cup (60 g) raisins

4 teaspoons dark rum

2 apples (Granny Smith or Braeburn)

4 tablespoons (60 g) butter

3 tablespoons sugar

1 teaspoon cinnamon

¼ teaspoon salt

1X basic batter

½ teaspoon vanilla extract

2 tablespoons (30 g) butter, melted

½ cup (50 g) sliced almonds

Confectioners' sugar, for serving

Method

1 Soak raisins in rum for 1 hour.

2 Peel apples, cut into quarters, remove seeds and finely dice.

3 In a pan, melt 4 tablespoons (60 g) butter. Stir in sugar, cinnamon, salt and diced apples and cook over low heat for 10 minutes, stirring until tender. Set aside.

4 Prepare basic batter (see page 8).

5 Drain and finely chop the raisins. Stir raisins and vanilla into the basic batter.

6 Heat ebelskiver pan over medium heat until hot. Pan is ready when a small amount of water sizzles when sprinkled over the pan.

7 Brush pan with a little butter and heat until it begins to bubble. Sprinkle a few sliced almonds into each well, then add 1 tablespoon of batter. Place 1 teaspoon apple filling in the center and seal with 1 teaspoon batter.

8 After 3 to 5 minutes, turn ebelskivers using wooden chopsticks or skewers and cook for another 2 to 3 minutes until browned on all sides. Repeat using all the batter, almonds and apple filling.

9 Serve warm dusted with confectioners' sugar.

Ebelskivers

WITH HERBS, GOAT CHEESE AND ROSEMARY HONEY

prep time 40 min
cooking time 20–25 min

makes 21 *ebelskivers*

3 tablespoons honey

3 sprigs rosemary

1 pinch chili pepper flakes

1X basic batter

3 tablespoons fresh parsley or basil, chopped

¼ cup (60 g) goat cheese

⅓ cup (60 g) tomatoes, diced

2 tablespoons (30 g) butter, melted

Method

1 In a saucepan, heat honey, rosemary sprigs and chili pepper flakes. Let stand for 20 minutes and then strain. Set aside.

2 Prepare basic batter (see page 8).

3 Fold chopped herbs into the basic batter using a rubber spatula.

4 Cut goat cheese into small cubes. In a bowl, combine cheese, diced tomatoes and 1 tablespoon rosemary honey.

5 Heat ebelskiver pan over medium heat until hot. Pan is ready when a small amount of water sizzles when sprinkled over the pan.

6 Brush pan with a little butter and heat until it begins to bubble. Spoon 1 tablespoon batter into each well. Place 1 teaspoon of the goat cheese-tomato mixture in the center and seal with 1 teaspoon batter.

7 After 3 to 5 minutes, turn ebelskivers using wooden chopsticks or skewers and cook for another 2 to 3 minutes until browned on all sides. Repeat using all the batter and goat cheese-tomato mixture.

8 Serve warm with rosemary honey.

BLACK FOREST
Ebelskivers
WITH WHIPPED CREAM

prep time 25 min
cooking time 18–24 min

makes 21 ebelskivers

1 jar preserved cherries

⅓ cup (75 g) sugar, divided

1 tablespoon cornstarch

8 teaspoons cherry brandy, divided

1 cup (125 g) unbleached all-purpose flour

½ teaspoon baking powder

¼ teaspoon salt

1 cup (240 ml) milk

4 tablespoons (60 g) butter, melted, divided

¾ cup (200 g) dark chocolate, melted, divided

2 large eggs, separated

1 cup (240 ml) heavy whipping cream

8 teaspoons cherry brandy

½ cup (50 g) dark chocolate, grated, for garnish

Method

1. In a saucepan, combine ¾ cup (200 ml) cherry juice and 3 tablespoons sugar and bring to a boil. Combine 1 tablespoon cornstarch with 2 tablespoons cold cherry juice and stir into saucepan to thicken. Stir in 4 teaspoons cherry brandy. Set aside.

2. Whisk together flour, baking powder and salt in a bowl. Stir in milk to make a smooth batter. Stir in 2 tablespoons melted butter and ⅓ cup (100 g) melted chocolate.

3. Separate the eggs and stir yolks into the batter. In a separate bowl, beat the egg whites until stiff peaks form. Add 1 tablespoon sugar and continue beating until the egg whites become glossy. Gently fold egg whites into batter using a rubber spatula.

4. Heat ebelskiver pan over medium heat until hot. Pan is ready when a small amount of water sizzles when sprinkled over the pan.

5. Brush pan with a little butter and heat until it begins to bubble. Spoon 1 tablespoon batter into each well. Place 1 teaspoon melted chocolate in the center and seal with 1 teaspoon batter.

6. After 3 to 5 minutes, turn ebelskivers using wooden chopsticks or skewers and cook for another 2 to 3 minutes until browned on all sides. Repeat using all the batter and remaining ingredients.

7. In a chilled bowl, whip the cream with 1 tablespoon sugar until stiff and stir in 4 teaspoons cherry brandy.

8. Serve ebelskivers with cherries, cherry brandy sauce, whipped cream and grated chocolate.

BLUE CHEESE-CRANBERRY
Ebelskivers
WITH PECAN CRUNCH

prep time 25 min
cooking time 18–24 min

makes 21 ebelskivers

2 tablespoons sugar
½ cup (60 g) pecans
½ cup (60 g) blue cheese, finely chopped
½ cup (60 g) dried cranberries, finely chopped
1 tablespoon honey
1X basic batter
2 tablespoons (30 g) butter, melted

Method

1 In a pan, heat sugar and stir until golden brown. Fold in pecans and transfer to a lightly greased plate. Let caramelized pecans cool and then chop finely.

2 Finely chop blue cheese and cranberries. Place in a bowl and mix with the honey.

3 Prepare basic batter (see page 8).

4 Fold chopped, caramelized pecans into the basic batter.

5 Heat ebelskiver pan over medium heat until hot. Pan is ready when a small amount of water sizzles when sprinkled over the pan.

6 Brush pan with a little butter and heat until it begins to bubble. Spoon 1 tablespoon batter into each well. Place 1 teaspoon of the blue cheese-cranberry mixture in the center and seal with 1 teaspoon batter.

7 After 3 to 5 minutes, turn ebelskivers using wooden chopsticks or skewers and cook for another 2 to 3 minutes until browned on all sides. Repeat using all the batter and blue cheese-cranberry filling.

8 Serve warm.

COCONUT MANGO
Ebelskivers

prep time 15 min
cooking time 18–24 min

makes 21 ebelskivers

1X basic batter, substitute 2 cups
   (480 ml) coconut milk for buttermilk

1 teaspoon vanilla extract

½ cup (50 g) shredded coconut

2 tablespoons sugar

1¼ cup (200 g) ripe mango, diced

2 tablespoons (30 g) butter, melted

Method

1. Prepare basic batter (see page 8) using 2 cups (480 ml) coconut milk instead of buttermilk and add 1 teaspoon vanilla extract.

2. Combine shredded coconut and sugar. Set aside.

3. Peel mango and cut into small cubes. Set aside.

4. Heat ebelskiver pan over medium heat until hot. Pan is ready when a small amount of water sizzles when sprinkled over the pan.

5. Brush pan with a little butter and heat until it begins to bubble. Add 1 teaspoon of the coconut-sugar mixture to each well and spoon in 1 tablespoon batter. Place 1 teaspoon diced mango in the center and seal with 1 teaspoon batter.

6. After 3 to 5 minutes, turn ebelskivers using wooden chopsticks or skewers and cook for another 2 to 3 minutes until browned on all sides. Repeat using all the batter and remaining ingredients.

7. Serve warm.

CHEESECAKE
Ebelskivers

prep time 15 min
cooking time 18–24 min

makes 21 ebelskivers

½ cup (45 g) graham cracker crumbs

3 teaspoons sugar

4 tablespoons (60 g) butter, melted, divided

6 ounces (185 g) cream cheese, softened

1 tablespoon confectioners' sugar

1 teaspoon lemon peel, finely grated

½ teaspoon vanilla extract

1X basic batter

Method

1 Combine graham cracker crumbs, sugar and 2 tablespoons butter. Set aside.

2 Combine cream cheese, confectioners' sugar, lemon peel and vanilla and mix well. Set aside.

3 Prepare basic batter (see page 8).

4 Heat ebelskiver pan over medium heat until hot. Pan is ready when a small amount of water sizzles when sprinkled over the pan.

5 Brush pan with a little of the remaining butter and heat until it begins to bubble. Add 1 teaspoon of the graham cracker mixture to each well and spoon in 1 tablespoon batter. Place 1 teaspoon cheesecake filling in the center and seal with 1 teaspoon batter.

6 After 3 to 5 minutes, turn ebelskivers using wooden chopsticks or skewers and cook for another 2 to 3 minutes until browned on all sides. Repeat using all the batter and remaining ingredients.

7 Serve warm.

CORN
Ebelskivers

WITH JALAPEÑO AND CHEDDAR

prep time 15 min
cooking time 24 min

makes 21 ebelskivers

⅔ cup (85 g) unbleached all-purpose flour

½ cup (80 g) cornmeal

½ teaspoon baking powder

¼ teaspoon salt

1 cup (240 ml) milk

4 tablespoons (60 g) butter, melted, divided

2 large eggs, separated

½ teaspoon sugar

1 jalapeño pepper, finely chopped

2 green onions, finely chopped

¾ cup (90 g) cheddar cheese, grated

¾ cup (120 g) canned corn, drained

Method

1 In a large bowl, whisk together the flour, cornmeal, baking powder and salt. Stir in milk to form a smooth batter. Stir in 2 tablespoons of butter.

2 Separate eggs and stir the yolks into the batter.

3 Beat the egg whites until stiff peaks form. Add sugar and continue beating until the egg whites become glossy. Gently fold egg whites into batter using a rubber spatula.

4 Remove seeds from jalapeño pepper and chop finely.

5 Finely chop the green onions.

6 Grate cheese and fold into the batter with the pepper, onions and corn.

7 Heat ebelskiver pan over medium heat until hot. Pan is ready when a small amount of water sizzles when sprinkled over the pan.

8 Brush pan with a little butter and heat until it begins to bubble. Spoon 2 tablespoons batter into each well.

9 After 3 to 5 minutes, turn ebelskivers using wooden chopsticks or skewers and cook for another 2 to 3 minutes until browned on all sides. Repeat using all the batter.

10 Serve warm with a spicy salsa.

[SHOWN IN THE NORDIC WARE EBELSKIVER PAN]

THAI-STYLE
Ebelskivers

WITH CHILI PEPPER-CUCUMBER DIP

prep time 25 min
cooking time 18−24 min

makes 21 ebelskivers

1¼ cups (150 g) unbleached all-purpose flour

½ teaspoon baking powder

½ teaspoon salt

1 cup (240 ml) milk

4 tablespoons (60 g) butter, melted, divided

2 large eggs, separated

½ teaspoon sugar

1 cup (250 g) cooked shrimp, peeled, diced

4 tablespoons fresh cilantro, chopped, divided

1 tablespoon fresh ginger, finely chopped

½ teaspoon chili pepper, seeded and finely chopped

¾ cup (200 ml) sweet chili sauce

½ cucumber, peeled, finely diced

Method

1 In a large bowl, whisk together the flour, baking powder and salt. Stir in milk to form a smooth batter. Stir in half of the butter.

2 Separate the eggs and stir yolks into the batter. Beat the egg whites until stiff peaks form. Add sugar and continue beating until the egg whites become glossy. Gently fold egg whites into the batter using a rubber spatula.

3 Finely dice peeled shrimp. Fold 2 tablespoons of the cilantro, all of the ginger, pepper and diced shrimp into the batter.

4 In a bowl, combine sweet chili sauce with 2 tablespoons cilantro.

5 Peel cucumber, cut in half lengthwise and scrape out seeds. Dice finely and stir into the chili sauce. Set aside.

6 Heat ebelskiver pan over medium heat until hot. Pan is ready when a small amount of water sizzles when sprinkled over the pan.

7 Brush pan with a little butter and heat until it begins to bubble. Spoon 2 tablespoons batter into each well.

8 After 3 to 5 minutes, turn ebelskivers using wooden chopsticks or skewers and cook for another 2 to 3 minutes until browned on all sides. Repeat using all the batter.

9 Serve warm with chili pepper cucumber dip.

POTATO
Ebelskivers

WITH BACON AND MUSHROOMS

prep time 40 min
cooking time 24 min

makes 21 ebelskivers

2 medium potatoes, to yield 2½ cups (300 g), grated

4 tablespoons (60 g) butter, melted, divided

⅔ cup (85 g) unbleached all-purpose flour

½ teaspoon baking powder

¼ teaspoon salt

1 cup (240 ml) milk

2 large eggs

½ teaspoon sugar

Nutmeg

Freshly ground black pepper, to taste

5–6 slices bacon

2 cups (130 g) mushrooms

1 tablespoon olive oil

1 garlic clove, chopped

1 tablespoon fresh tarragon, chopped

¼ cup (50 g) mascarpone

Method

1 Cook the potatoes in boiling salted water until just tender, about 20 minutes. Let cool. Peel and grate the potatoes and toss with 2 tablespoons of butter. Set aside.

2 In a large bowl, whisk together the flour, baking powder and salt. Stir in milk to form a smooth batter. Stir grated potatoes into the batter. Separate the eggs and stir yolks into the batter.

3 In a medium bowl, beat the egg whites until stiff peaks form. Add sugar and continue beating until they become glossy. Gently fold egg whites into the batter with a rubber spatula. Season with a pinch of nutmeg and pepper.

4 Cut bacon into finely chopped pieces. Cut mushrooms into thin slices.

5 In a pan, heat olive oil and sauté mushrooms. Stir in garlic, tarragon and mascarpone and cook for about 5 to 7 minutes. Season to taste with salt and pepper.

6 Heat ebelskiver pan over medium heat until hot. Pan is ready when a small amount of water sizzles when sprinkled over the pan.

7 Brush pan with a little butter and heat until it begins to bubble. Place several pieces of bacon in each well and spoon 1 tablespoon batter on top. Place 1 teaspoon of the mushroom mixture in the center and seal with 1 teaspoon batter.

8 After 3 to 5 minutes, turn ebelskivers using wooden chopsticks or skewers and cook for another 2 to 3 minutes until browned on all sides. Repeat using all the batter and remaining ingredients. Serve warm.

LEMON-FILLED

Ebelskiver

DOUGHNUTS

prep time 10 min
cooking time 30 min

makes 21 doughnuts

½ cup (160 g) prepared lemon curd (1 10-oz jar)

1¾ cups (210 g) unbleached all-purpose flour

¾ teaspoon baking soda

1 teaspoon baking powder

1½ tablespoons sugar

2 teaspoons lemon zest, finely grated

3 large eggs, separated

1¾ cups (420 ml) buttermilk, shaken

7 tablespoons (105 g) butter, melted

Confectioners' sugar, for serving

Method

1 In a small bowl, mix lemon curd until light and smooth.

2 In a large bowl, whisk togther the flour, baking soda, baking powder, sugar and lemon zest.

3 In a small bowl, lightly beat the egg yolks and stir in the buttermilk.

4 Add the yolk mixture to the flour mixture, whisking until well combined.

5 In a medium bowl, beat the egg whites until stiff peaks form. Gently fold the egg whites into the batter with a rubber spatula.

6 Heat ebelskiver pan over medium heat until hot. Pan is ready when a small amount of water sizzles when sprinkled over the pan.

7 Brush pan with a little butter and heat until it begins to bubble. Spoon 1 tablespoon of batter into each cup. Place 1 teaspoon lemon curd in the center (push lemon curd down in the batter using a chopstick) and seal with 1 teaspoon of batter. Cook until edges appear brown and center is bubbly.

8 Cook until the bottoms are golden brown and crispy. Rotate each doughnut about every 30 seconds using wooden chopsticks or skewers until browned on all sides. Repeat using all the batter and remaining ingredients.

9 Dust with confectioners' sugar and serve.

DANISH

Ebelskiver

DOUGHNUTS WITH APRICOT JAM

prep time 15 min
cooking time 24 min

makes 21 *doughnuts*

3 large eggs, separated

2 cups (480 ml) buttermilk, shaken

1½ cups (180 g) unbleached all-purpose flour

2 teaspoons baking powder

1 tablespoon sugar

½ teaspoon salt

¼ teaspoon ground cinnamon

6 tablespoons (90 g) butter, melted, divided

½ cup (160 g) apricot jam

Confectioners' sugar, for serving

Method

1 In a medium bowl, beat egg whites until stiff peaks form. Set aside. In a separate mixing bowl, beat the egg yolks and buttermilk together.

2 Whisk together the dry ingredients and add to buttermilk mixture. Add 3 tablespoons butter and stir together until smooth. Gently fold in the beaten egg whites.

3 Heat ebelskiver pan over medium heat until hot. Pan is ready when a small amount of water sizzles when sprinkled over the pan.

4 Brush pan with a little butter and heat until it begins to bubble. Spoon 1 tablespoon of batter into each cup. Wait for batter to bubble. Add 1 teaspoon apricot jam. Seal with 1 teaspoon of batter.

5 Cook until the bottoms are golden brown and crispy. Rotate each doughnut about every 30 seconds using wooden chopsticks or skewers until browned on all sides. Repeat using all the batter and jam.

6 Dust with confectioners' sugar and serve warm.

Note

Any favorite jam can be used. Add 1 teaspoon of raspberry, strawberry or blackberry jam to each cup after batter is bubbling.

BLUEBERRY AND RICOTTA CHEESE

Ebelskiver

DOUGHNUTS

prep time **15 min**
cooking time **28 min**

makes 28 doughnuts

- 1¾ cups (210 g) unbleached all-purpose flour
- ¾ teaspoon baking soda
- 1 teaspoon baking powder
- 2 tablespoons sugar
- ½ teaspoon salt
- 2 teaspoons lemon zest, finely grated
- 3 egg yolks
- 1⅓ cups (320 ml) buttermilk, shaken
- ¾ cup (190 g) ricotta cheese
- 5 egg whites
- 3 tablespoons (45 g) butter, melted
- 1 pint (300 g) blueberries, rinsed and patted dry
- Confectioners' sugar, for serving

Method

1 In a large bowl, whisk together the flour, baking soda, baking powder, sugar, salt and lemon zest. Set aside.

2 In a separate bowl, lightly whisk the egg yolks. Stir in the buttermilk and ricotta cheese.

3 Make a well in the flour mixture. Stir the egg yolk mixture into the flour mixture. Mix until well combined and set aside.

4 In another bowl, beat the egg whites until stiff peaks form. Gently fold the egg whites into the batter with a rubber spatula.

5 Heat ebelskiver pan over medium heat until hot. Pan is ready when a small amount of water sizzles when sprinkled over the pan.

6 Brush pan with a little butter and heat until it begins to bubble. Spoon 1 tablespoon of batter into each cup. Place 3 or 4 blueberries in the center of the batter and seal with 1 teaspoon of batter. Do not overfill the cups.

7 Cook until the bottoms are golden brown and crispy. Rotate each doughnut about every 30 seconds using wooden chopsticks or skewers until browned on all sides. Repeat using all the batter and blueberries.

8 Dust with confectioners' sugar. Serve warm.

Ebelskiver

DOUGHNUTS WITH GLAZE

prep time 15 min
cooking time 24 min

makes 21 doughnuts

FOR GLAZE

2 tablespoons (30 g) butter

1 cup (120 g) confectioners' sugar

½ teaspoon vanilla

2 tablespoons water (clear glaze) or milk (white glaze)

FOR DOUGHNUTS

2 large eggs, separated

1 tablespoon sugar

½ teaspoon baking powder

1 cup (125 g) unbleached all-purpose flour

Salt

1 cup (240 ml) milk

2 tablespoons (30 ml) vegetable oil

5 tablespoons (75 g) butter, melted

Method

For Glaze

1 Melt butter and add to confectioners' sugar, vanilla and water. Mix well. Pour into shallow dish and set aside for dipping warm doughnuts.

For Doughnuts

1 In a medium bowl, beat egg yolks until light and fluffy. Stir in sugar.

2 Sift dry ingredients together with a pinch of salt. Add the dry ingredients to the egg mixture, alternating with the milk. Stir in the oil.

3 In a separate bowl, beat the egg whites until stiff peaks form. Gently fold into the batter using a rubber spatula.

4 Heat ebelskiver pan over medium heat until hot. Pan is ready when a small amount of water sizzles when sprinkled over the pan.

5 Brush pan with a little butter and heat until it begins to bubble. Add about 2 tablespoons of batter to each cup.

6 Cook until the bottoms are golden brown and crispy. Rotate each doughnut about every 30 seconds using wooden chopsticks or skewers until browned on all sides. Repeat using all the batter.

7 Dip in glaze and serve.

PUMPKIN SPICE
Ebelskiver
DOUGHNUTS

prep time 15 min
cooking time 35 min

makes 35 *doughnuts*

2¼ cups (280 g) unbleached all-purpose flour

2 teaspoons baking powder

1 tablespoon sugar

2 teaspoons cinnamon

¼ teaspoon nutmeg

¼ teaspoon cloves

½ teaspoon baking soda

½ teaspoon salt

3 large eggs, separated

½ cup (125 g) pumpkin purée

4 tablespoons (60 g) butter, melted

2 cups (480 ml) buttermilk, shaken

Vegetable oil, for pan

Confectioners' sugar, for serving

Method

1 In a large bowl, whisk dry ingredients together. In a separate bowl, stir egg yolks, pumpkin purée, butter and buttermilk together until well-blended. Gradually add wet ingredients to flour mixture and stir well to combine.

2 Beat the egg whites until stiff peaks form. Gently fold egg whites into the batter using a rubber spatula.

3 Heat ebelskiver pan over medium heat until hot. Pan is ready when a small amount of water sizzles when sprinkled over the pan.

4 Brush pan with a little oil and heat until it begins to bubble. Add about 2 tablespoons of batter to each cup. Cook until edges appear brown and center is bubbly.

5 Rotate each doughnut about every 30 seconds using wooden chopsticks or skewers until browned on all sides. Repeat using all the batter.

6 Roll in confectioners' sugar and serve.

LEMON DROP
Ebelskiver
DOUGHNUTS

prep time 15 min
cooking time 18–24 min

makes 21 ebelskivers

1½ cups (180 g) unbleached all-purpose flour

1 cup (200 g) sugar, divided

2 teaspoons baking powder

¼ teaspoon salt

1 large egg

½ cup (120 ml) milk

4 tablespoons (60 g) butter, melted

½ teaspoon vanilla

1 tablespoon lemon zest, finely grated

1 tablespoon lemon juice

Vegetable oil, for pan

Sugar

Method

1 Combine flour, ½ cup (100 g) sugar, baking powder and salt in a bowl and mix well.

2 In another bowl, beat egg and blend with milk, melted butter, vanilla, lemon zest and lemon juice. Add flour mixture and stir just to moisten.

3 Heat ebelskiver pan over medium heat until hot. Pan is ready when a small amount of water sizzles when sprinkled over the pan.

4 Place 1 teaspoon of oil in each well of pan. Spoon 2 tablespoons batter into each well.

5 Cook until the bottoms are golden brown and crispy. Rotate each doughnut about every 30 seconds using wooden chopsticks or skewers until browned on all sides. Remove and drain on paper towels. Repeat using all the batter.

6 Roll hot ebelskivers in sugar and serve.

STATE FAIR
Ebelskiver
DOUGHNUTS

prep time **40 min**
cooking time **20–25 min**

makes 35 ebelskivers

2 cups (250 g) unbleached all-purpose flour

1½ tsp baking powder

1 cup (200 g) sugar, divided

¼ teaspoon salt

1 large egg

¼ cup (60 ml) vegetable oil, plus extra for pan

¾ cup (180 ml) milk

2 tsp cinnamon

Method

1 Sift flour and baking powder in a large bowl. Add ½ cup (100 g) sugar and salt and mix well.

2 In another bowl, lightly beat egg and add ¼ cup (60 ml) oil.

3 Mix in flour mixture until crumbly. Stir in milk.

4 Leave the dough in the mixing bowl in a warm place to rest for about 30 minutes.

5 Mix ½ cup (100 g) sugar together with cinnamon in a shallow bowl. Set aside.

6 Heat ebelskiver pan over medium heat until hot. Pan is ready when a small amount of water sizzles when sprinkled over the pan.

7 Place 1 teaspoon of oil in each well of pan. Spoon 2 tablespoons batter into each well.

8 Cook until the bottoms are golden brown and crispy. Rotate each doughnut about every 30 seconds using wooden chopsticks or skewers until browned on all sides. Remove and place on paper towels. Repeat using all the batter.

9 Roll hot ebelskivers in cinnamon-sugar mixture and serve.

Pancakes

Pancakes

WITH BANANAS, BLUEBERRIES AND WHIPPED CREAM

prep time 15 min
cooking time 20 min

servings 4

FOR WHIPPED CREAM

1 cup (240 ml) heavy whipping cream

1 tablespoon sugar

½ teaspoon vanilla extract

FOR PANCAKES

2 cups (250 g) unbleached all-purpose flour

2 tablespoons sugar

½ teaspoon salt

1 teaspoon baking powder

½ teaspoon baking soda

2 cups (480 ml) buttermilk, shaken

¼ cup (60 g) sour cream

2 large eggs

3 tablespoons (45 g) butter, melted

Vegetable oil

2 ripe bananas, sliced, for garnish

1 cup (150 g) fresh blueberries, for garnish

Confectioners' sugar, for serving

Method

For Whipped Cream

1 Whip cream in a chilled bowl until it begins to thicken. Add sugar and vanilla. Continue whipping until stiff peaks form. Chill until needed.

For Pancakes

1 In a large bowl, whisk together flour, sugar, salt, baking powder and baking soda.

2 In a separate bowl, whisk together buttermilk, sour cream, eggs and butter.

3 Make a well in the center of flour mixture and pour in the wet ingredients and gently stir until just combined. Do not over mix. Allow batter to sit for 10 minutes before cooking.

4 Heat a griddle or nonstick skillet over medium heat for 4 to 5 minutes. Brush lightly with vegetable oil. Pour ¼ cup (60 ml) of batter for each pancake onto hot griddle. Cook until edges are set and bubbles appear on top, about 2 to 3 minutes. Flip pancakes and cook until second side is golden brown, 1 to 2 minutes longer. Repeat using all the batter.

5 Serve pancakes immediately with sliced bananas, blueberries and a dollop of whipped cream. Dust with confectioners' sugar.

Pancakes

WITH MAPLE YOGURT AND RASPBERRIES

prep time 10 min
cooking time 18 min

servings 4

FOR MAPLE YOGURT TOPPING

2 cups (500 g) plain yogurt

¼ cup (60 ml) maple syrup

FOR PANCAKES

2 cups (250 g) unbleached all-purpose flour

2 teaspoons baking powder

1 teaspoon baking soda

2 tablespoons sugar

½ teaspoon salt

2 large eggs

2¼ cups (540 ml) buttermilk, shaken

2 tablespoons (30 g) butter, melted

1 cup (150 g) fresh raspberries

Vegetable oil, for pan

Method

For Maple Yogurt Topping

1 Combine yogurt and maple syrup in a bowl and mix well. Set aside.

For Pancakes

1 In a large bowl, whisk together the flour, baking powder, baking soda, sugar and salt.

2 In a separate bowl, whisk together the eggs, buttermilk and butter.

3 Make a well in the center of the flour mixture and slowly add wet ingredients. Whisk until just combined. Do not over mix.

4 Heat a griddle or nonstick skillet over medium heat for 4 to 5 minutes. Brush lightly with vegetable oil. Pour ¼ cup (60 ml) of batter for each pancake onto hot griddle. Cook until edges are set and bubbles appear on top, about 2 to 3 minutes. Flip pancakes and cook until second side is golden brown, 1 to 2 minutes longer. Repeat using all the batter.

5 Serve pancakes hot with yogurt topping and fresh raspberries.

BUTTERMILK
BUG
Pancakes

prep time 5 min
cooking time 2 min

makes 14 *pancakes*

1 cup (125 g) unbleached all-purpose flour

1 teaspoon baking soda

½ teaspoon salt

1 large egg, lightly beaten

½ cup (120 ml) milk

1 cup (240 ml) buttermilk, shaken

Vegetable oil, for pan

Method

1 In a large bowl, mix flour, baking soda, salt, egg, milk and buttermilk until smooth.

2 Brush the Bug Pancake Pan with oil and place over medium heat. Heat pan over medium heat 4 to 5 minutes.

3 Carefully pour batter into each bug mold. Do not overfill. Cook, turning once, until golden, about 2 minutes per batch. Repeat using all the batter.

4 Serve immediately with a favorite topping.

[SHOWN IN THE NORDIC WARE BACKYARD BUGS PANCAKE PAN]

BLUEBERRY
Pancakes
WITH STRAWBERRIES

prep time 10 min
cooking time 20 min

servings 4

2 cups (250 g) unbleached all-purpose flour

½ teaspoon baking soda

½ teaspoon baking powder

½ teaspoon salt

2 tablespoons sugar

2 large eggs

½ cup (120 ml) buttermilk, shaken

1¼ cup (300 ml) milk

3 tablespoons (45 g) butter, melted

1 cup (150 g) fresh blueberries, plus extra for garnish

Vegetable oil, for pan

1 cup (150 g) fresh strawberries, for garnish

Method

1 In a large bowl, whisk together the flour, baking soda, baking powder, salt and sugar.

2 In a separate bowl, lightly beat the eggs. Add the buttermilk and milk and mix to combine.

3 Make a well in the center of flour mixture and pour in the wet ingredients and gently stir until just combined. Do not over mix. Stir in the butter and gently fold in the blueberries.

4 Heat a griddle or nonstick skillet over medium heat for 4 to 5 minutes. Brush lightly with vegetable oil. Pour ¼ cup (60 ml) of batter for each pancake onto hot griddle. Cook until edges are set and bubbles appear on top, about 2 to 3 minutes. Flip pancakes and cook until second side is golden brown, 1 to 2 minutes longer. Repeat using all the batter.

5 Serve immediately with butter and maple syrup. Garnish with fresh blueberries and sliced strawberries.

POTATO
Pancakes
WITH BACON AND ONIONS

prep time 15 min
cooking time 28 min

servings 2

5 slices bacon

2 tablespoons (30 g) butter, divided

1 large onion, chopped, divided

1 teaspoon caraway seeds, optional

Salt, to taste

3 cups (650 g) cold mashed potatoes

1 large egg

2 tablespoons unbleached all-purpose flour

Method

1 In a large nonstick skillet or griddle over medium heat, cook bacon until crisp. Drain, reserving 1 tablespoon of bacon fat. Crumble the bacon and set aside.

2 Heat the bacon fat with 1 tablespoon of butter. Add chopped onion, reserving 2 tablespoons, and the caraway seeds. Season with salt. Cook, stirring frequently, until onions are browned, about 8 to 10 minutes. Transfer to a small bowl, cover and keep warm.

3 Mix potatoes, egg, remaining onions and crumbled bacon in a bowl until well-combined. Sprinkle flour on wax paper. Form six pancakes with the potato mixture. Lightly coat both sides with flour.

4 Melt remaining butter in skillet or griddle over medium heat. Cook pancakes for about 4 minutes per side, until pancakes are lightly browned.

5 Set pancakes on paper towels to wick away excess oil. Transfer to a serving platter. Serve with the cooked onion topping.

BUTTERMILK
Pancakes
WITH CHERRY JAM

prep time 30 min
cooking time 45 min

servings 4

FOR CHERRY JAM

2 pounds (900 g) fresh cherries

2 lemons

1¾ cups (350 g) sugar

FOR BUTTERMILK PANCAKES

1 cup (125 g) unbleached all-purpose flour

1 tablespoon sugar

1 teaspoon baking powder

1 teaspoon baking soda

½ teaspoon salt

1 large egg

1 cup (240 ml) buttermilk

Vegetable oil, for pan

Method

For Cherry Jam

1 Remove the pits and stems from all the cherries and chop half of them. Place all the cherries in a medium-sized, heavy-bottomed pan. Grate the zest from one lemon and add to the pan. Cut both lemons in half and squeeze all the juice into the pan. Place the pan over medium-high heat and stir until it simmers. Reduce heat to low. Cover and simmer for about 15 to 20 minutes. Stir frequently. When the fruit is soft, add 1¾ cups sugar and stir well to combine.

2 Increase the heat to a simmer. Cook uncovered, for about 6 to 8 minutes. The jam will thicken as it simmers. The jam is done when it coats the back of a cool, metal spoon. Remove from heat and let cool. Transfer the jam to glass jars. Cover and store in the refrigerator. The cherry jam will keep for up to 3 weeks.

For Buttermilk Pancakes

1 In a large bowl, whisk together the flour, sugar, baking powder, baking soda and salt. In a small bowl, lightly beat the egg with the buttermilk. Add the wet ingredients to the flour mixture and mix until just blended.

2 Heat a griddle or nonstick skillet over medium heat for 4 to 5 minutes. Brush the hot griddle lightly with vegetable oil. Pour ¼ cup (60 ml) batter for each pancake onto hot griddle. When bubbles rise on the top of the pancakes, flip and cook until golden brown on the second side. Repeat using all the batter.

3 Serve immediately with cherry jam topping.

ORANGE
Pancakes
WITH MAPLE SYRUP

prep time 10 min
cooking time 18 min

servings 4–6

2 cups (250 g) unbleached all-purpose flour

½ teaspoon salt

½ teaspoon baking soda

1½ teaspoons baking powder

¼ cup (50 g) sugar

5 tablespoons (75 g) butter, melted

¾ cup (180 ml) orange juice

2 tablespoons orange zest, finely grated

¼ cup (60 ml) milk

¾ cup (180 ml) buttermilk, shaken

3 large eggs

Vegetable oil, for pan

2 oranges, sliced

Maple syrup, to serve

Method

1 In a large bowl, whisk together the flour, salt, baking soda, baking powder and sugar.

2 In a separate bowl, whisk together the butter, orange juice, orange zest, milk, buttermilk and eggs until well blended.

3 Make a well in the center of the flour mixture and slowly pour in the orange-buttermilk mix. Whisk gently until just combined. Do not over mix.

4 Heat a griddle or nonstick skillet over medium heat for 4 to 5 minutes. Brush lightly with vegetable oil. Pour ¼ cup (60 ml) of batter for each pancake onto hot griddle. Cook until edges are set and bubbles appear on top, about 2 to 3 minutes. Flip pancakes and cook until second side is golden brown, 1 to 2 minutes longer. Repeat using all the batter.

5 Divide hot pancakes among plates and serve with orange slices and maple syrup.

ZOO ANIMAL
Pancakes

prep time 10 min
cooking time 3 min

makes 14 pancakes

½ cup (60 g) unbleached all-purpose flour

½ tablespoon sugar

¼ teaspoon baking soda

¾ cup (180 ml) buttermilk, shaken

1 tablespoon vegetable oil

1 large egg

½ teaspoon vanilla extract

Vegetable oil, for pan

Method

1   In a large bowl, whisk together the flour, sugar and baking soda.

2   In a separate bowl, whisk together the buttermilk, oil, egg and vanilla until blended.

3   Make a well in the center of the flour mixture and slowly add the wet ingredients. Blend until just moistened. Let stand 5 minutes.

4   Brush the Zoo Animal Pan with oil and place over medium heat. Heat pan over medium heat 4 to 5 minutes.

5   Carefully pour batter into each zoo animal mold. Do not overfill. Cook, turning once, until golden, about 2 minutes per batch. Repeat using all the batter.

6   Serve hot with a favorite topping.

[SHOWN IN THE NORDIC WARE ZOO ANIMAL PANCAKE PAN]

POTATO AND LEEK
Pancakes

prep time 25 min
cooking time 18 min

servings 2–4

5 large potatoes

3 large leeks, trimmed

3 tablespoons (45 g) butter, divided

Salt, to taste

Freshly ground black pepper, to taste

2 large eggs, lightly beaten

2 teaspoons fresh thyme, or 1 teaspoon dried

1 tablespoon unbleached all-purpose flour

3 tablespoons olive oil

Method

1 Peel and finely grate potatoes. Wrap in cheesecloth and twist to squeeze out any liquid. Let stand for several minutes and squeeze dry again. Set aside.

2 Slice the white and pale green parts of the leek into small rings. Melt 1 tablespoon butter in a medium skillet. Add leeks and stir until softened by not browned, about 5 to 7 minutes. Season with salt and pepper and set aside.

3 In a large bowl, combine all ingredients, except remaining butter and oil. Mix well until potatoes and leeks are well coated.

4 Heat a griddle or nonstick skillet over medium heat for 4 to 5 minutes. Add butter and oil to coat the pan. Working in small batches, drop heaping tablespoons of potato mixture onto the griddle. Use the back of a spoon to flatten. Cook 2 to 3 minutes per side, until golden brown and crisp. Drain on paper towels.

5 Repeat using all the potato mixture, adding more butter and oil to the griddle, if needed. Season with salt and pepper to taste and serve hot.

Pancakes

WITH BLUEBERRIES AND GRAPES

prep time 15 min
cooking time 20 min

servings 4

2½ cups (300 g) unbleached all-purpose flour

4 tablespoons sugar

1½ tablespoons baking powder

1 teaspoon salt

1 egg

2¼ cups (540 ml) milk

2 tablespoons (30 g) butter, melted

Vegetable oil, for pan

1 cup (150 g) fresh blueberries, for garnish

1 bunch green grapes, for garnish

Maple syrup, for serving

Method

1 In a large bowl, whisk together the flour, sugar, baking powder and salt.

2 In a separate bowl, whisk together the egg and milk.

3 Make a well in the center of the flour mixture and slowly add the wet ingredients. Whisk gently until just combined. Add melted butter and blend.

4 Heat a griddle or nonstick skillet over medium heat. Brush lightly with vegetable oil. Pour ¼ cup (60 ml) of batter onto hot griddle. Cook until edges are set and bubbles appear on top, about 2 to 3 minutes. Flip pancakes and cook until second side is golden brown, 1 to 2 minutes longer.

5 Divide among plates. Garnish with blueberries and grapes. Serve hot with butter and maple syrup.

Waffles

ALMOND

Waffles
WITH CRANBERRY-POACHED PEARS

prep time 30 min
cooking time 30 min

servings 4

FOR CRANBERRY-POACHED PEARS

4 small pears, peeled with stems intact

2 tablespoons sugar

1 cinnamon stick

1 strip each lemon and orange peels, 4-in long

4 tablespoons honey

1 teaspoon lemon juice

2¾ cups (280 g) fresh cranberries

½ teaspoon vanilla extract

FOR ALMOND WAFFLES

1½ cups (180 g) unbleached all-purpose flour

½ cup (60 g) almond flour

2 tablespoons sugar

2 teaspoons baking powder

1 teaspoon baking soda

¾ teaspoon salt

2 cups (480 ml) buttermilk, shaken

6 tablespoons (90 g) butter, melted

2 large eggs

2 teaspoons almond extract

Cooking spray or oil

Sweetened whipped cream, for garnish

Method

For Cranberry-Poached Pears

1 Place pears snugly in a small saucepan. Add enough water to cover. Add sugar, cinnamon stick, citrus peels, honey and lemon juice. Bring to a boil and stir to dissolve sugar. Reduce heat and simmer until the pears are tender, about 10 minutes. Add cranberries and simmer for about 3 minutes, until soft and keep their shape. Stir in vanilla. Transfer to a dish and let cool. Cover and refrigerate overnight. Remove cinnamon stick and citrus peels before serving.

For Waffles

1 In a large bowl, whisk together flour, almond flour, sugar, baking powder, baking soda and salt. In a separate bowl, whisk together buttermilk, butter, eggs and almond extract. Gradually whisk liquid ingredients into flour mixture until just combined.

2 Preheat waffle pan or iron and coat lightly with cooking spray or oil. Pour batter into each waffle mold. Cook waffles until golden brown and cooked through, about 3 to 4 minutes. Repeat using all the batter.

3 Divide waffles between plates and serve with halved pears. Spoon cranberries and syrup on top of the pears and garnish with whipped cream.

LEMON  WITH LEMON CREAM AND STRAWBERRIES

prep time 25 min
cooking time 15 min

servings 4

FOR LEMON CREAM

¾ CUP (180 ML) HEAVY WHIPPING CREAM

3 tablespoons confectioners' sugar

1 teaspoon lemon zest, finely grated

3 ounces (85 g) cream cheese, softened

FOR STRAWBERRIES

1 pint (300 g) fresh strawberries

1 tablespoon sugar

FOR LEMON WAFFLES

4 eggs, separated

¼ cup (50 g) sugar

½ teaspoon salt

1 cup (240 ml) milk

1 tablespoon lemon juice

1 tablespoon lemon zest, finely grated

4 tablespoons (60 g) butter, melted

1¼ cups (160 g) unbleached all-purpose flour

½ teaspoon baking powder

Cooking spray or oil

Method

For Lemon Cream and Strawberries

1 Add whipping cream, confectioners' sugar, lemon zest and cream cheese to a chilled bowl. Beat on high speed until mixture becomes soft and fluffy. Chill until needed.

2 Remove stems from the strawberries. Sprinkle with sugar and crush with a fork. Allow to sit for about 10 minutes.

For Lemon Waffles

1 In a medium bowl, beat egg yolks with sugar and salt. Blend in milk, lemon juice, lemon zest and butter.

2 Sift in the flour and baking powder. Stir until just blended.

3 Beat the egg whites until stiff peaks form. Gently fold the egg whites into the batter with a rubber spatula.

4 Preheat waffle pan or iron and coat lightly with cooking spray or oil. Pour batter into each waffle mold. Cook waffles until golden brown and cooked through, about 3 to 4 minutes. Repeat using all the batter.

5 Serve waffles hot with lemon cream and strawberries.

SOUR CREAM  WITH RASPBERRIES AND WHIPPED CREAM

prep time 20 min
cooking time 15 min

servings 4–6

FOR WHIPPED CREAM

1 cup (240 ml) heavy whipping cream

3 tablespoons confectioners' sugar

½ TEASPOON VANILLA EXTRACT

FOR SOUR CREAM WAFFLES

3 large eggs, separated

¾ cup (180 ml) milk

8 tablespoons (120 g) butter, melted

¾ cup (170 g) sour cream

1½ cups (180 g) unbleached all-purpose flour

½ teaspoon baking soda

2 teaspoons baking powder

¼ cup sugar

Cooking spray or oil

1 pint (300 g) fresh raspberries

1 ounce (30 g) bittersweet chocolate, shaved

Method

For Whipped Cream

1 Whip cream in a chilled bowl until it begins to thicken. Add sugar and vanilla. Continue whipping until stiff peaks form. Chill until needed.

For Sour Cream Waffles

1 In a small bowl, beat the egg whites until stiff peaks form. Set aside.

2 In a large bowl, beat the egg yolks with a whisk. Beat in the milk, butter and sour cream. In a separate bowl, sift the dry ingredients together. Add dry ingredients to the milk mixture and mix until just blended. Using a rubber spatula, gently fold in the egg whites.

3 Preheat waffle pan or iron and coat lightly with cooking spray or oil. Pour batter into each waffle mold. Cook waffles until golden brown and cooked through, about 3 to 4 minutes. Repeat using all the batter.

4 Garnish with whipped cream, fresh raspberries and shaved chocolate and serve.

BELGIAN

Waffles

prep time 10 min
cooking time 5 min

servings 6

2 cups (250 g) unbleached all-purpose flour

1 tablespoon baking powder

1 teaspoon salt

3 tablespoons sugar

4 large eggs, separated

1¼ (300 ml) cups milk

½ cup (120 ml) vegetable oil

Cooking spray or oil

Method

1 In a large bowl, whisk together the flour, baking powder, salt and sugar.

2 In a separate bowl, whisk together the egg yolks, milk and oil.

3 Make a well in the center of the dry ingredients. Pour the egg mixture into the well. Blend the wet and dry ingredients together until just moistened.

4 In a small bowl, beat the egg whites until stiff peaks form. Gently fold the egg whites into the waffle batter. Do not over mix.

5 Preheat waffle pan or iron and coat lightly with cooking spray or oil. Pour batter into each waffle mold. Cook waffles until golden brown and cooked through, about 3 to 4 minutes. Repeat using all the batter.

6 Serve warm with a favorite topping.

[SHOWN IN THE NORDIC WARE BELGIAN WAFFLER]

BELGIAN

Waffles
WITH SLICED FRUIT AND MAPLE SYRUP

prep time 15 min
rising time 1 h
cooking time 20 min

servings 8

2¼ teaspoons active dry yeast

3 cups (720 ml) warm milk, divided

3 eggs, separated

¾ cup (170 g) butter (1½ sticks), melted

½ cup (100 g) sugar

½ teaspoon salt

2 teaspoons (10 ml) vanilla extract

4 cups (500 g) unbleached all-purpose flour

Cooking spray or oil

2 cups (300 g) fresh strawberries trimmed and halved

1 cup (150 g) fresh blueberries

2 nectarines, sliced

Maple syrup, to serve

Method

1 In a small bowl, dissolve yeast in ¼ cup (60 ml) warm milk.

2 In a separate bowl, beat egg whites until stiff peaks form and set aside.

3 In a large bowl, mix together the egg yolks, ¼ cup (60 ml) milk, butter and sugar. Add the yeast mixture, salt and vanilla and blend well.

4 Gradually add flour and 2 cups milk, alternating between the two. Gently fold the egg whites into the waffle batter.

5 Cover the batter with plastic wrap and place in a warm place to rise until it doubles in size, about 1 hour.

6 Preheat waffle pan or iron and coat lightly with cooking spray or oil. Pour batter into each waffle mold. Cook waffles until golden brown and cooked through, about 3 to 4 minutes. Repeat using all the batter.

7 Divide waffles among plates. Garnish with fresh fruit. Drizzle with maple syrup and serve.

BELGIAN

Waffle

COOKIES

prep time 15 min
chilling time 12 h
cooking time 20 min

2 cups (500 g) unbleached all-purpose flour

1 cup (125 g) whole wheat flour

¾ cup (170 g) butter (1½ sticks), softened

6 large eggs

2½ cups (550 g) dark brown sugar, packed

½ cup (100 g) sugar

½ cup (120 ml) milk

2 tablespoons vanilla extract

2 tablespoons rum

2 tablespoons whiskey

½ cup (85 g) chocolate chips

Cooking spray or oil

Confectioners' sugar, for serving

Method

1 In a bowl, whisk together the all-purpose and whole wheat flour.

2 In a separate large bowl, blend together the butter, eggs, brown sugar, sugar, milk, vanilla, rum and whiskey. Mix well. Slowly add flour mixture one cup at a time until all the flour is added.

3 Fold in chocolate chips.

4 Preheat the waffle or cookie iron and coat lightly with cooking spray or oil. Place about 1 tablespoon of dough in the center of each section of the waffle iron. Cook waffle cookies until golden brown and cooked through, about 1 to 3 minutes. Repeat using all the dough.

5 Transfer immediately to a wire rack. Dust with confectioners' sugar if desired, once cookies are cool.

Tips

If alcohol-free cookies are preferred, substitute water. Yield will depend on type of waffle iron used. Can be frozen in airtight containers.

CARAMEL APPLE
Waffles

prep time 25 min
cooking time 30 min

servings 4

FOR CARAMELIZED APPLES

6 tablespoons (90 g) butter

⅓ cup (75 g) brown sugar

2 pounds Golden Delicious apples

⅔ cup (160 ml) heavy whipping cream

FOR SPICED WAFFLES

¾ cup (90 g) unbleached all-purpose flour

2 tablespoons whole wheat flour

6 tablespoons sugar

1½ teaspoons baking powder

1¼ teaspoons ground ginger

½ teaspoon ground cinnamon

¼ teaspoon baking soda

¼ teaspoon salt

⅛ teaspoon ground coriander

⅛ teaspoon ground nutmeg

¼ teaspoon ground cloves

¾ cup (180 ml) buttermilk, shaken

2 tablespoons honey

1 large egg, separated

½ teaspoon orange zest, finely grated

2 tablespoons (30 g) butter, melted

Cooking spray or oil

Vanilla bean ice cream

Method

For Caramelized Apples

1 Melt the butter in a large skillet over medium heat. Slowly add sugar, stirring until the sugar dissolves, about 1 to 2 minutes.

2 Peel the apples and cut into ½-inch cubes. Add apples to the sugar and sauté until the apples are golden brown and tender, about 10 minutes. Add cream and simmer until sauce is slightly thickened, about 2 to 3 minutes. Set aside. Apples can be reheated prior to serving.

For Spiced Waffles

1 In a large bowl, whisk together the dry ingredients. In a separate bowl, whisk together the buttermilk, honey, egg yolk and orange zest. Whisk buttermilk mixture into dry ingredients. Stir in butter.

2 In a separate bowl, beat egg white until stiff peaks form and gently fold into batter.

3 Preheat waffle pan or iron and coat lightly with cooking spray or oil. Pour batter into each waffle mold. Cook waffles until golden brown and cooked through, about 3 to 4 minutes. Repeat using all the batter.

4 To serve, divide waffles among plates. Garnish with caramelized apples and a scoop of ice cream.

Waffles

WITH RASPBERRY SAUCE AND FRESH FRUIT

prep time 20 min
cooking time 30 min

servings 6

FOR RASPBERRY SAUCE

1 pint (300 g) fresh raspberries

¼ cup (50 g) sugar

2 tablespoons orange juice

2 tablespoons cornstarch

1 cup (240 ml) cold water

FOR WAFFLES

2 large eggs

1¾ cups (420 ml) milk

½ cup (120 ml) vegetable oil

1 teaspoon vanilla extract

2 cups (250 g) unbleached all-purpose flour

1 tablespoon sugar

4 teaspoons baking powder

¼ teaspoon salt

Cooking spray or oil

¾ cup (100 g) fresh blueberries

¾ cup (100 g) fresh raspberries

¾ cup (100 g) fresh strawberries, sliced

Method

For Raspberry Sauce

1 In a saucepan, combine raspberries, sugar and orange juice. Whisk the cornstarch and cold water together until smooth and add to the saucepan. Bring to a boil, stirring to dissolve the sugar.

2 Reduce heat and simmer for about 5 minutes, stirring constantly. The sauce will thicken as it cools. Purée the sauce using a handheld blender.

3 Strain through a fine mesh sieve. Raspberry sauce will keep refrigerated up to 2 weeks in an airtight container.

For Waffles

1 In a large bowl, beat eggs until light and fluffy. Add milk, oil and vanilla, mixing well. In a separate bowl, sift dry ingredients together. Add dry ingredients to the milk mixture and mix until just blended.

2 Preheat waffle pan or iron and coat lightly with cooking spray or oil. Pour batter into each waffle mold. Cook waffles until golden brown and cooked through, about 3 to 4 minutes. Repeat using all the batter.

3 To serve, divide waffles among plates, top with raspberry sauce and fresh fruit.

 Waffles

WITH WHIPPED CREAM AND STRAWBERRIES

prep time 25 min
cooking time 15 min

servings 4

FOR WHIPPED CREAM

1 cup (240 ml) heavy whipping cream

3 tablespoons confectioners' sugar

½ teaspoon vanilla extract

FOR WAFFLES

1½ cups (180 g) unbleached all-purpose flour

2 tablespoons cornmeal

1 teaspoon salt

½ teaspoon baking soda

2 large eggs, separated

1¾ cups (420 ml) buttermilk

4 tablespoons (60 g) butter, melted

Cooking spray or oil

1 pint (300 g) fresh strawberries

Method

For Whipped Cream

1 Whip cream in a chilled bowl until it begins to thicken. Add sugar and vanilla. Continue whipping until stiff peaks form. Chill until needed.

For Waffles

1 In a large bowl, whisk together flour, cornmeal, salt and baking soda.

2 In a separate bowl, whisk the egg yolk, buttermilk and melted butter.

3 In another bowl, beat egg whites until stiff peaks form.

4 Slowly add the buttermilk mixture to the dry ingredients, mixing with a rubber spatula. Gently fold in the egg whites.

5 Preheat waffle pan or iron and coat lightly with cooking spray or oil. Pour batter into each waffle mold. Cook waffles until golden brown and cooked through, about 3 to 4 minutes. Repeat using all the batter.

6 To serve, divide waffles among plates, top with a generous dollop of whipped cream, fresh strawberries and dust with confectioners' sugar.

PUMPKIN

Waffles

prep time 10 min
cooking time 15 min

servings 4

1½ cups (180 g) unbleached all-purpose flour

1 tablespoon baking powder

½ teaspoon baking soda

1 teaspoon ground cinnamon

1 teaspoon ground nutmeg

1 teaspoon ground ginger

½ teaspoon salt

2 large eggs

¼ cup (50 g) light brown sugar

1 cup (250 g) canned pumpkin purée

1⅔ (400 ml) cups milk

4 tablespoons (60 g) butter, melted

Cooking spray or oil

Butter, to serve

Method

1 In a large bowl, whisk together flour, baking powder, baking soda, cinnamon, nutmeg, ginger and salt.

2 In a separate bowl, add eggs, brown sugar, pumpkin, milk and butter. Beat well. Gently fold pumpkin mixture into the flour mixture.

3 Preheat waffle pan or iron and coat lightly with cooking spray or oil. Pour batter into each waffle mold. Cook waffles until golden brown and cooked through, about 3 to 4 minutes. Repeat using all the batter.

4 Serve hot with butter.

Waffles

WITH BUTTER AND MAPLE SYRUP

prep time 15 min
cooking time 15 min

servings 3

2 cups (250 g) unbleached all-purpose flour

2 tablespoons sugar

2 teaspoons baking powder

1 teaspoon baking soda

¾ teaspoon salt

2 cups (480 ml) buttermilk, shaken

6 tablespoons (90 g) butter, melted

2 large eggs

2 teaspoons vanilla extract

Cooking spray or oil

Butter, to serve

Maple syrup, to serve

Method

1 In a large bowl, whisk together flour, sugar, baking powder, baking soda and salt.

2 In a separate bowl, whisk together buttermilk, butter, eggs and vanilla. Gradually mix into the flour mixture until just combined.

3 Preheat waffle pan or iron and coat lightly with cooking spray or oil. Pour batter into each waffle mold. Cook waffles until golden brown and cooked through, about 3 to 4 minutes. Repeat using all the batter.

4 Divide hot waffles among plates. Serve with butter and maple syrup.

[SHOWN ON THE NORDIC WARE MINI WAFFLE PANCAKE PAN]

CHOCOLATE, CHOCOLATE CHIP

Waffles

WITH WHIPPED CREAM

prep time 20 min
cooking time 15 min

servings 4

FOR WHIPPED CREAM

1 cup (240 ml) heavy whipping cream

3 tablespoons confectioners' sugar

½ TEASPOON VANILLA EXTRACT

FOR THE WAFFLES

1¼ cup (160 g) unbleached all-purpose flour

¾ cup (150 g) sugar

1 teaspoon salt

1 teaspoon baking powder

1 large egg, lightly beaten

¼ cup (60 ml) canola oil

1 cup (240 ml) buttermilk, shaken

3 tablespoons unsweetened cocoa

½ cup (85 g) chocolate chips

½ teaspoon vanilla

½ teaspoon baking soda

½ teaspoon white vinegar

Cooking spray or oil

Method

For Whipped Cream

1 Whip cream in a chilled bowl until it begins to thicken. Add sugar and vanilla. Continue whipping until stiff peaks form. Chill until needed.

For Chocolate, Chocolate Chip Waffles

1 In a large bowl, whisk together flour, sugar, salt and baking powder.

2 Add egg, oil and buttermilk and mix until smooth.

3 Add cocoa and chocolate chips to waffle batter and mix. Add vanilla, baking soda and vinegar, in that order, and beat until everything is well mixed, about 2 minutes.

4 Preheat waffle pan or iron and coat lightly with cooking spray or oil. Pour batter into each waffle mold. Cook waffles until golden brown and cooked through, about 3 to 4 minutes. Repeat using all the batter.

5 Serve hot with whipped cream.

Eggs

Omelet
WITH PEPPERS AND ONIONS

prep time 10 min
cooking time 10 min

serving 1

1 teaspoon butter

2 tablespoons red bell pepper, sliced

½ sweet onion, sliced

1 clove garlic, minced

2 large eggs

2 tablespoons water

1 tablespoon fresh parsley, chopped

2 teaspoons fresh thyme, chopped

2 tablespoons sharp cheddar cheese

Freshly ground black pepper, to taste

Method

1 Heat butter on a griddle over medium heat. Add bell pepper, onion and garlic. Sauté until tender for about 3 minutes. Set aside. Increase heat to medium-high.

2 In a small bowl, whisk together eggs, water, parsley and thyme.

3 Pour egg mixture onto the griddle. Eggs should start to set immediately at the edges. Gently move eggs so all portions cook evenly. When eggs have set, sprinkle the cheese over them. Add pepper and onion mixture. Fold omelet in half and slide omelet onto a serving plate.

4 Season with freshly ground black pepper. Serve immediately.

SCRAMBLED

Eggs

WITH HOME-FRIED POTATOES

prep time 15 min
cooking time 40 min

servings 2

FOR HOME-FRIED POTATOES

2½ tablespoons peanut oil, divided

1 large onion, chopped

3 medium potatoes, scrubbed, cubed

1½ tablespoons butter

Salt, to taste

Freshly ground black pepper, to taste

FOR EGGS

4 large eggs

2 tablespoons milk

Salt, to taste

Freshly ground black pepper, to taste

1 tablespoon butter

Method

For Home-Fried Potatoes

1 Heat 1 tablespoon of peanut oil on a griddle over medium-high heat until hot but not smoking. Add the chopped onions and stir until lightly browned about 8 to 10 minutes. Transfer the onions to a small bowl and set aside.

2 Cut the potatoes into medium-sized cubes and place in a large saucepan. Cover with 1 inch of water and season with salt. Bring to a boil and cook for about 8 minutes. Remove from heat and drain thoroughly in a colander.

3 Heat the butter and 1½ tablespoons oil on the griddle over medium-high heat until the butter begins to bubble. Add the potatoes and arrange in a single layer, using a spatula. Cook without stirring for about 4 to 5 minutes, until golden brown. Carefully turn the potatoes and arrange again in a single layer, cooking until golden brown. Repeat turning until the potatoes are tender and golden brown on most sides, about 10 minutes. Add the onions and season to taste with salt and pepper.

For the Eggs

1 Keep the griddle over medium-high heat. In a medium bowl, whisk the eggs and add milk, salt and pepper. Melt 1 tablespoon butter on the griddle and add the eggs. Reduce heat to low and stir gently until the eggs begin to set. Taste for seasoning.

2 Divide potatoes and eggs between plates and serve immediately.

Omelets

WITH POTATOES, CHEDDAR AND SMOKED HAM

prep time 12 min
cooking time 18 min

servings 2

1 large potato, peeled and diced

Salt, to taste

6 large eggs

2 tablespoons milk

Freshly ground black pepper, to taste

2 tablespoons (30 g) butter, divided

3 green onions, chopped

½ cup baby spinach leaves

4 slices smoked ham

2 ounces (60 g) cheddar cheese, grated

Cooking spray

Method

1 Place the diced potatoes in a large saucepan, cover with 1 inch of water and season with salt. Bring to a boil and cook for about 5 to 6 minutes. Remove from heat and drain thoroughly in a colander.

2 In a medium bowl, whisk together the eggs and milk until fully blended. Season with salt and pepper. Set aside.

3 Melt 1 tablespoon butter in a skillet over medium-high heat. Add the potatoes and cook until lightly browned but not crisp, about 4 to 5 minutes. Add remaining butter, chopped green onion and baby spinach leaves. Cook until the spinach is just wilted. Remove from heat and set aside.

4 Preheat the Omelet/Frittata Pan over medium heat. Spray each side of the pan with cooking spray. Ladle half of the beaten eggs into both sides of the omelet pan. Fill pan no more than ¾ full to avoid overflow. Cook until the eggs begin to set, about 2 minutes.

5 Spoon half of the potato mixture over the top of the eggs on one or both sides of the pan. Add 2 slices of ham and half of the grated cheese. Following the instructions for the folding pan, lift one side of the pan and fold it over the other side, combining the two omelet halves. Keep the pan folded closed and cook for an additional minute.

6 Slide the finished omelet out of the pan onto a serving plate and keep warm. Repeat for the second omelet. Serve warm.

[SHOWN IN THE NORDIC WARE OMELET/FRITTATA PAN]

Omelet

ROLLS WITH HERB CREAM CHEESE

prep time 10 min
cooking time 10 min

servings 2

4 large eggs

4 tablespoons milk

Salt, to taste

Freshly ground black pepper, to taste

Nutmeg, freshly grated

1¾ cups (400 g) cream cheese, softened

2 tablespoons fresh parsley, chopped

1 tablespoon fresh dill, chopped

1 tablespoon fresh chives, chopped

2 tablespoons Parmesan cheese, grated

1 tablespoon butter

Method

1 Whisk the eggs and milk together and season with salt, pepper and nutmeg.

2 Mix the cream cheese with the chopped herbs and the grated cheese until smooth and creamy. Season to taste with salt and pepper.

3 Heat the butter on a griddle or skillet over medium heat. Pour half of the egg mixture onto the griddle. Eggs should start to set immediately at the edges. Gently move eggs so all portions cook evenly. Once cooked, remove the omelet from pan and spread with the herb cream cheese.

4 Repeat making another omelet and spreading with the herb cream cheese. Roll up each omelet, slice at an angle and serve immediately.

Eggs
AND BACON SANDWICH ON A BAGEL

prep time 3 min
cooking time 1 min

serving 1

1–2 large eggs

1 tablespoon milk

Salt, to taste

Freshly ground black pepper, to taste

1 bagel, split in half

2–3 slices precooked bacon

1 slice cheddar cheese

Method

1 Crack 1 or 2 eggs into the bottom portion of the Egg 'n Muffin Pan. Add milk and stir gently with a fork. Season with salt and pepper. Microwave for 1 minute. Cooking time may vary depending on microwave.

2 Meanwhile, toast the bagel.

3 Place bacon and cheese on half of the bagel. Lift eggs out of the egg cooker and place on bagel. Top with other half and serve hot.

Eggs
IN A BASKET WITH FRESH FRUIT AND YOGURT

prep time 10 min
cooking time 6 min

servings 4

1 cup (150 g) fresh blueberries

1 cup (150 g) fresh raspberries

1 cup (150 g) fresh strawberries, sliced

4 slices whole wheat bread

Butter

4 large eggs

Salt, to taste

Freshly ground black pepper, to taste

¼ cup (25 g) sliced almonds

1 cup (250 g) yogurt

Method

1 Combine fresh fruit in a bowl and set aside.

2 Butter bread slices on both sides. Using a small glass or cookie cutter, cut a 2-inch hole in the middle of each slice of bread.

3 Preheat griddle over medium heat. Place buttered bread on the griddle. Add a small teaspoon of butter into the center of the bread.

4 Crack an egg into a small bowl and gently pour into the hole. Repeat with eggs and the remaining slices of bread. Season with salt and pepper.

5 When the eggs begin to set around the edges of the hole, flip the bread with the eggs and finish cooking the eggs.

6 Serve with fresh fruit garnished with sliced almonds and a spoonful of yogurt.

Omelets

WITH ASPARAGUS AND FETA CHEESE

prep time 10 min
cooking time 15 min

servings 2

6 large eggs

2 tablespoons milk

1 tablespoon fresh thyme, chopped

2 tablespoons green onion, chopped

Salt, to taste

Freshly ground black pepper, to taste

½ pound (230 g) fresh asparagus, trimmed and cut into thirds

2 ounces (60 g) feta cheese, crumbled

Cooking spray or oil

Method

1 In medium bowl, whisk together the eggs and milk. Stir in chopped thyme and onions, salt and pepper. Set aside.

2 Arrange prepared asparagus in a large microwave-safe bowl, adding 2 tablespoons water. Cover with vented plastic wrap and microwave on high for 2 minutes. Stir and cook for 2 additional minutes. Asparagus should be tender-crisp. Drain and pat dry. Set aside.

3 Heat nonstick griddle coated with cooking spray or oil over medium heat. Pour half of egg mixture onto griddle. Cook for 2 to 3 minutes until the bottom just begins to set.

4 Sprinkle with half of crumbled feta cheese. Add half of the asparagus. Cook for additional 4 to 5 minutes until the eggs have almost set.

5 Fold the omelet in half, using a large heat-proof spatula. Cook for about 3 minutes until the cheese is melted and the omelet is golden. Slide onto plate and keep warm.

6 Coat griddle with cooking spray or oil again and repeat with remaining egg mixture, cheese and asparagus.

7 Serve warm.

[SHOWN ON THE NORDIC WARE FLATTOP REVERSIBLE GRILL GRIDDLE]

Omelets

WITH HONEY FRUIT SALAD

prep time 15 min
cooking time 6 min

servings 2

FOR HONEY FRUIT SALAD

2 fresh kiwis, peeled and sliced

1 cup (150 g) fresh strawberries, trimmed and sliced

1 ripe mango, peeled, pitted and sliced

3 tablespoons honey

2 teaspoons lemon juice

FOR OMELET

6 large eggs

2 tablespoons orange juice

Salt, to taste

Freshly ground black pepper, to taste

Cooking spray

2 sprigs mint or lemon balm, for garnish

Method

For Honey Fruit Salad

1 In a large bowl, combine the peeled and sliced fruit. Drain liquid from fruit before using.

2 In a small bowl, whisk together the honey and lemon juice. Pour honey mixture over fruit and gently toss to coat.

For Omelet

1 In medium bowl, whisk together the eggs and orange juice. Season with salt and pepper.

2 Preheat Omelet/Frittata Pan over medium heat. Spray each side of pan with cooking spray. Ladle half of the eggs into both sides of omelet pan. Fill no more than ¾ full to avoid overflow. Cook until eggs begin to set, about 2 minutes.

3 Spoon half of the fruit over top of eggs on one side of pan. Following the instructions for folding pan, lift one side of the pan and fold it over the other side, combining the two omelet halves. Keep the pan folded closed and cook for an additional minute.

4 Slide the finished omelet out of the pan onto a serving plate and keep warm. Repeat for the second omelet. Serve garnished with mint or lemon balm.

Eggs

'N MUFFIN WITH CANADIAN BACON AND CHEESE

prep time 2 min
cooking time 2 min

serving 1

1–2 large eggs

1 tablespoon milk

Salt, to taste

Freshly ground black pepper, to taste

2 slices Canadian bacon

1 English muffin, split

1 slice cheddar cheese

Method

1 Crack 1 or 2 eggs into the bottom portion of the Egg 'n Muffin Pan. Add milk and stir gently with a fork. Season with salt and pepper. Place the bacon on top of eggs and microwave for 1 minute. Cooking time may vary depending on microwave.

2 Toast English muffin.

3 Place cheese on top of eggs and bacon. Microwave for about 15 seconds. Lift eggs out of egg cooker and place on muffin. Serve.

[SHOWN IN THE NORDIC WARE EGG 'N MUFFIN PAN]

BANANA
French Toast

prep time 5 min
cooking time 10 min

servings 3

2 large eggs

⅔ cup (160 ml) milk

¼ teaspoon ground cinnamon

1 teaspoon vanilla extract

Salt

2 ripe bananas

6 slices bread, thick slices

Maple syrup, to serve

Method

1 In a medium bowl, beat eggs, milk, cinnamon, vanilla and a pinch of salt together.

2 Mash 1 banana and add to the egg mixture.

3 Heat a lightly oiled griddle over medium-high heat.

4 Place each slice of bread into the egg-banana mixture. Turn once and coat both sides. Place on the griddle and cook each side until golden brown.

5 Transfer to plates. Garnish with banana slices. Serve hot with maple syrup.